JAZZ GUITAR WORKSHOP

12 KEY JAZZ GUITAR WORKOUT

MAJOR
&
MELODIC MINOR
EDITION

By Robert Green

1st Edition October 2013

Print Edition ISBN 978-1-937187-07-1
eBook Edition ISBN 978-1-937187-08-8

Library of Congress Control Number: 2013921440

Musical Score : Jazz
Musical Score : Studies & exercises, etudes

Layout and music engraving by Robert Green
Cover Design by Robert Green

Foreward

Jazz Guitar Workshop - 12 Key Jazz Guitar Workout
Major and Melodic Minor Edition

Jazz Guitar wood shedding exercises in 12 keys -
The Major scales modes and arpeggios over 2 octaves in 12 keys.
Diatonic triads, diatonic 7th chords, broken thirds, sequences, triadic and 7th chord permutations.
Melodic Minor scales, modes and arpeggios over 2 octaves in 12 keys.
including Lydian Dominant, Augmented (maj #5), Diminished Whole tone (alt Dom) Locrian #2 (min7b5)
Diatonic triads, diatonic 7th chords, broken thirds, sequences, triadic and 7th chords permutations.

These technique building exercises can be incorporated into a daily practice routine focusing on instrumental facility and ear training while internalising the harmonic function of the scales, modes and their related arpeggios.

One of the most important aspects of learning any instrument is being able to set aside time to practice.
As a wise instructor once said, " there's no magic powder ".
Great players worked hard to get there, if it is your wish and your intention, you can get there too.
For the advanced student, practice the book in 12 keys, for the beginning to intermediate student practice the exercises in one key to gain familiarity with the instrument.
When the exercises become comfortable move to another key until all keys are comfortable.
Scale studies are designed to help the guitarist to learn the fingerboard while building dexterity, flexibilty, stamina as well as building muscle memory and training the ear.

Table of Contents.

Table of contents.

Part 1. Scale studies in the key of C Major

Scales, Modes and Arpeggios over 2 octaves

C Major scale

C maj7 arpeggio

D Dorian scale

D min 7 arpeggio

E Phrygian scale

E min 7 arpeggio

F Lydian scale

F maj 7 arpeggio

G Mixolydian scale

G 7 arpeggio

A Aeolian scale

A min7 arpeggio

B Locrian scale

B min7 b5 arpeggio

4 Note Scale Groupings

The following exercise outlines the use of 4 note groupings moving stepwise diatonically through the scale of C major.

For example, the 4 note grouping starts on the root note or 1st degree of the scale and progresses stepwise. The exercise then descends from the 2nd octave C back to the root.

Ascending

Descending

Permutation 2

Up & Down

As in the previous exercise the following exercise outlines the use of 4 note groupings moving stepwise diatonically through the scale of C major.

Notice in exercise #2 the 4 note grouping starts on the root note or 1st degree of the scale and progresses stepwise. In this example we descend when we hit the 5th note in the sequence eg. descending from the 2nd 4 note grouping.

Ascending

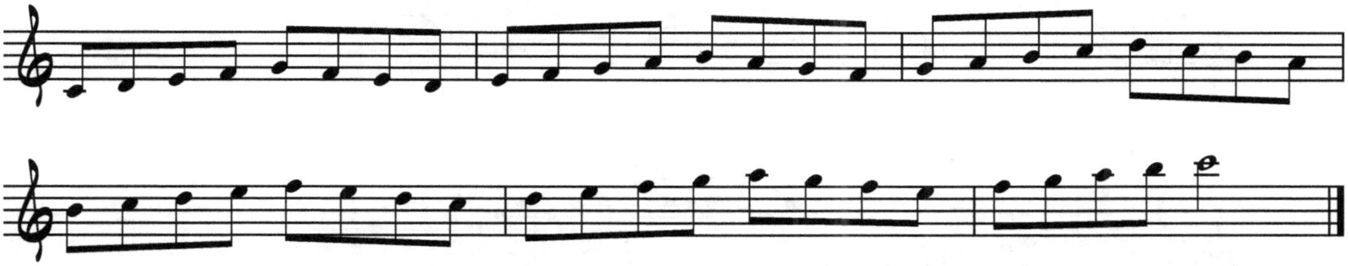

Descending

Broken Thirds

Ascending

Descending

3 Note Groupings

C major scale in triplet groupings
Ascending

Descending

Diatonic 7th Chords in Triplets

C major arpeggio

D min7 arpeggio

E min7 arpeggio

F maj 7 arpeggio

G 7 arpeggio

A min7 arpeggio

B min7 b5 arpeggio

C major arpeggio

4 Note Groupings Diatonic Triads

Ascending 1351

Descending 1351

Ascending 1531

Descending 1531

4 Note Groupings Diatonic 7th Chords

Ascending

Descending

4 Note Groupings Diatonic 7th Chords

Permutation 2
Ascending & descending

Permutation 3

Down the chord stepwise up the scale

Scale studies in the key of Db Major

Scales, Modes and Arpeggios over 2 octaves

Db Major scale

Db maj7 arpeggio

Eb Dorian scale

Eb min7 arpeggio

F Phrygian scale

F min7 arpeggio

Gb Lydian scale

Gb maj7   arpeggio

Ab Mixolydian scale

Ab7 arpeggio

Bb Aeolian scale

Bb min7 arpeggio

C Locrian scale

C min7 b5 arpeggio

4 Note Scale Groupings

The following exercise outlines the use of 4 note groupings moving stepwise diatonically through the scale of Db major.
For example, the 4 note grouping starts on the root note or 1st degree of the scale and progresses stepwise. The exercise then descends from the 2nd octave Db back to the root.

Ascending

Descending

Permutation 2

Up & Down

As in the previous exercise the following exercise outlines the use of 4 note groupings moving stepwise diatonically through the scale of Db major.

Notice in exercise #2 the 4 note grouping starts on the root note or 1st degree of the scale and progresses stepwise. In this example we descend when we hit the 5th note in the sequence eg. descending from the 2nd 4 note grouping.

Ascending

Descending

Broken Thirds

Ascending

Descending

3 Note Groupings

Db major scale in triplet groupings
Ascending

Descending

Diatonic 7th Chords in Triplets

Db major arpeggio

Eb min7 arpeggio

F min7 arpeggio

Gb maj 7 arpeggio

Ab 7 arpeggio

Bb min7 arpeggio

C min7 b5 arpeggio

Db major arpeggio

4 Note Groupings Diatonic Triads

Ascending 1351

Descending 1351

Ascending 1531

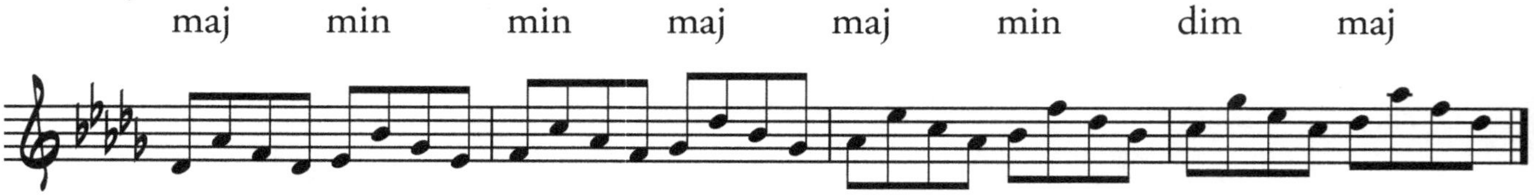

Descending 1531

4 Note Groupings Diatonic 7th Chords

Ascending

maj7 min7 min7 maj7 dom7 min7 half dim maj7

min7 min7 maj7 dom7 min7 half dim maj7

Descending

maj7 half dim min7 dom7 maj7 min7 min7 maj7

half dim min7 dom7 maj7 min7 min7 maj7

Permutation 2
Ascending & descending

maj7 min7 min7 maj7 dom7 min7 half dim maj7

half dim min7 dom7 maj7 min7 min7 maj7

Permutation 3

Down the chord stepwise up the scale

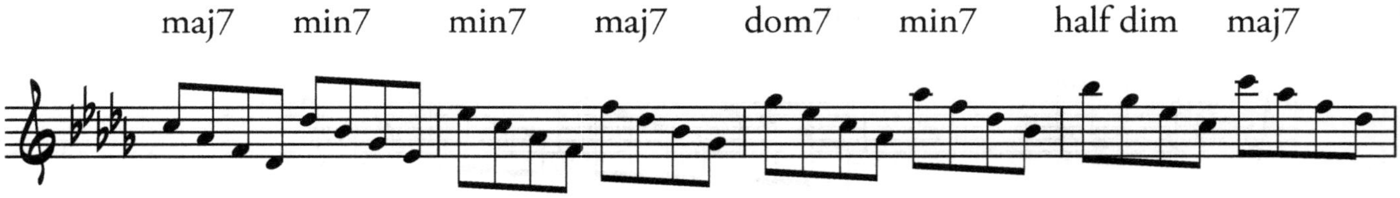

Scale studies in the key of D Major

Scales, Modes and Arpeggios over 2 octaves

D Major 7 scale

D maj 7 arpeggio

E Dorian scale

E min7 arpeggio

F# Phrygian scale

F# min7 arpeggio

G Lydian scale

G maj 7 arpeggio

A Mixolydian scale

A dom7 arpeggio

B Aeolian scale

B min7 arpeggio

C# Locrian scale

C# min7 b5 arpeggio

4 Note Scale Groupings

The following exercise outlines the use of 4 note groupings moving stepwise diatonically through the scale of D major.

For example, the 4 note grouping starts on the root note or 1st degree of the scale and progresses stepwise. The exercise then descends from the 2nd octave D back to the root.

Ascending

Descending

Permutation 2

Up & Down

As in the previous exercise the following exercise outlines the use of 4 note groupings moving stepwise diatonically through the scale of D major.

Notice in exercise #2 the 4 note grouping starts on the root note or 1st degree of the scale and progresses stepwise. In this example we descend when we hit the 5th note in the sequence eg. descending from the 2nd 4 note grouping.

Ascending

Descending

Broken Thirds

Ascending

Descending

3 Note Groupings

D major scale in triplet groupings

Ascending

Descending

Diatonic 7th Chords in Triplets

D maj arpeggio

E min7 arpeggio

F# min7 arpeggio

G maj 7 arpeggio

A 7 arpeggio

B min7 arpeggio

C# min7 b5 arpeggio

D major arpeggio

4 Note Groupings Diatonic Triads

Ascending 1351

Descending 1351

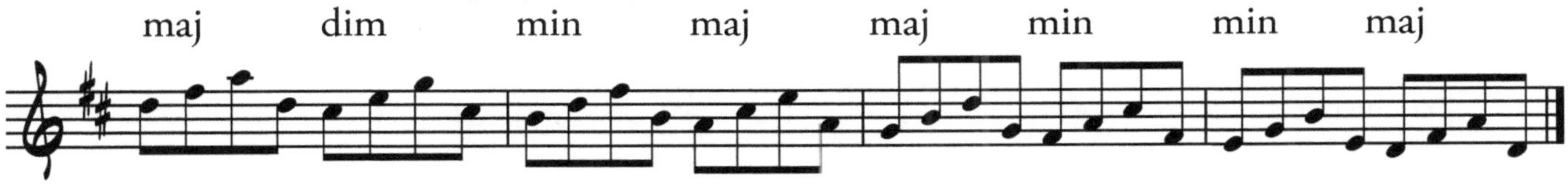

Ascending 1531

Descending 1531

4 Note Groupings Diatonic 7th chords

Ascending

Descending

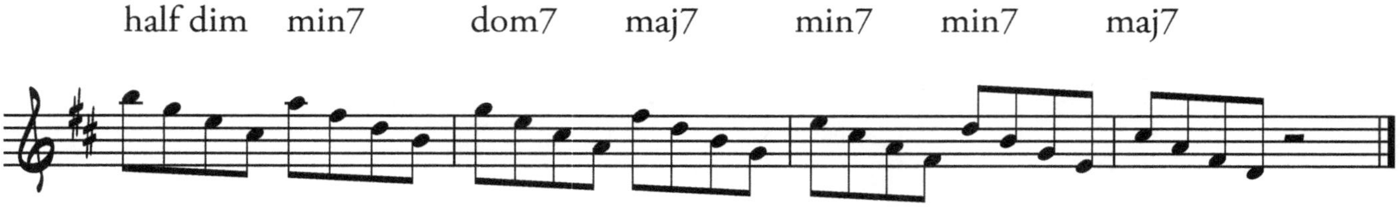

Permutation 2
Ascending & descending

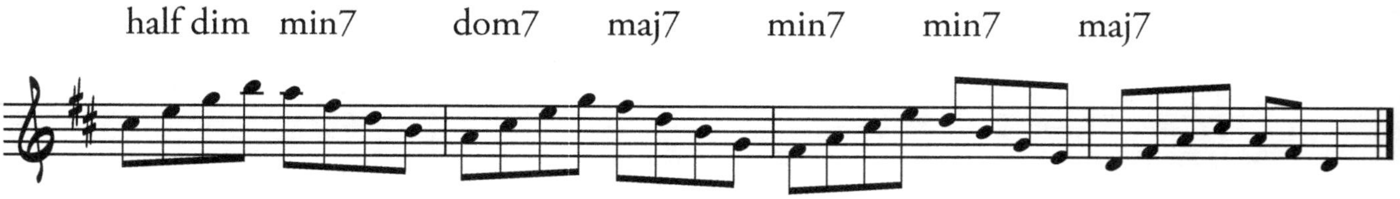

Permutation 3

Down the chord stepwise up the scale

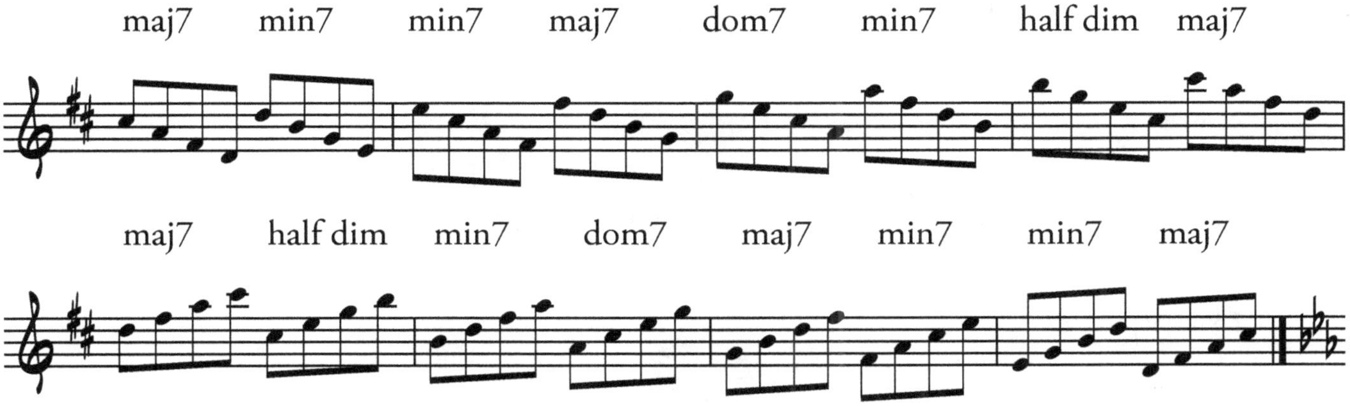

Scale studies in the key of Eb Major

Scales, Modes and Arpeggios over 2 octaves

Eb Major scale

Eb maj 7 arpeggio

F Dorian scale

F min 7 arpeggio

G Phrygian scale

G min 7 arpeggio

Ab Lydian scale

Ab maj 7 arpeggio

Bb Mixolydian scale

Bb7 arpeggio

C Aeolian scale

C min7 arpeggio

D Locrian scale

D min7 b5 arpeggio

4 Note Scale Groupings

The following exercise outlines the use of 4 note groupings moving stepwise diatonically through the scale of Eb major.
For example, the 4 note grouping starts on the root note or 1st degree of the scale and progresses stepwise. The exercise then descends from the 2nd octave Eb back to the root.

Ascending

Descending

Permutation 2

Up & Down

As in the previous exercise the following exercise outlines the use of 4 note groupings moving stepwise diatonically through the scale of Eb major.

Notice in exercise #2 the 4 note grouping starts on the root note or 1st degree of the scale and progresses stepwise. In this example we descend when we hit the 5th note in the sequence eg. descending from the 2nd 4 note grouping.

Ascending

Descending

Broken Thirds

Ascending

Descending

3 Note Groupings

Eb major scale in triplet groupings

Ascending

Descending

Diatonic 7th Chords in Triplets

Eb maj arpeggio

F min7 arpeggio

G min7 arpeggio

Ab maj 7 arpeggio

Bb 7 arpeggio

C min7 arpeggio

D min7 b5 arpeggio

Eb maj arpeggio

4 Note Groupings Diatonic Triads

Ascending 1351

Descending 1351

Ascending 1531

Descending 1531

4 Note Groupings Diatonic 7th Chords

Ascending

Descending

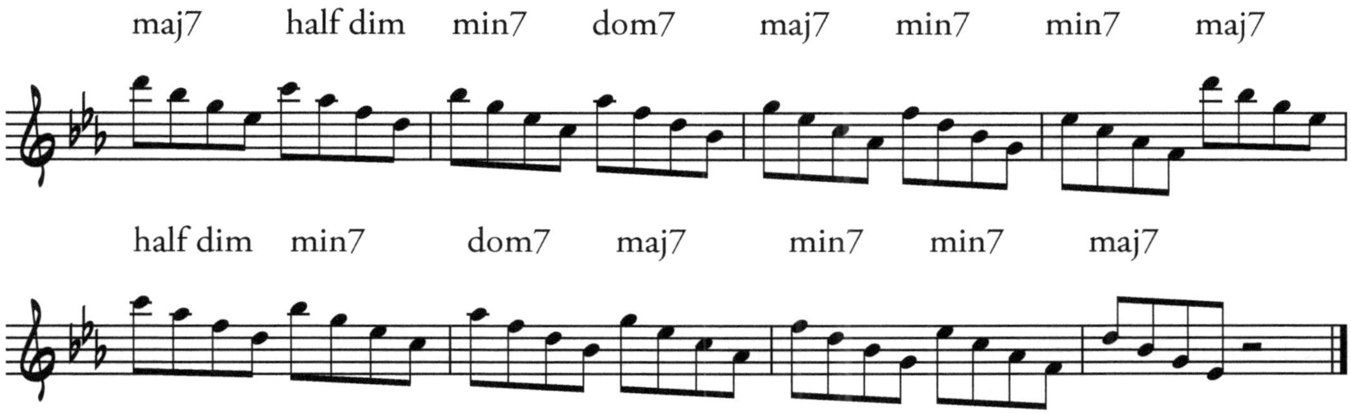

Permutation 2
Ascending & descending

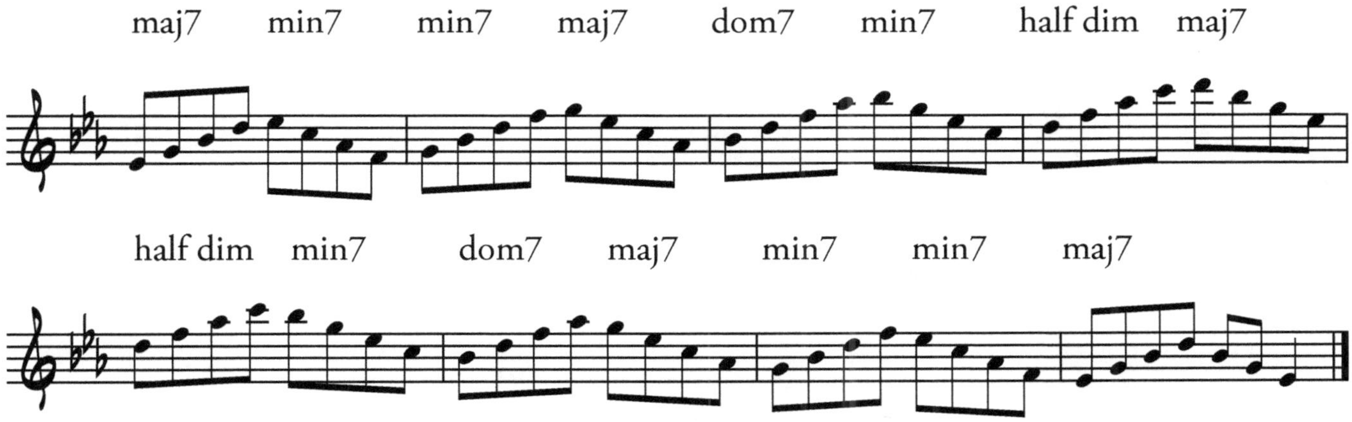

Permutation 3

Down the chord stepwise up the scale

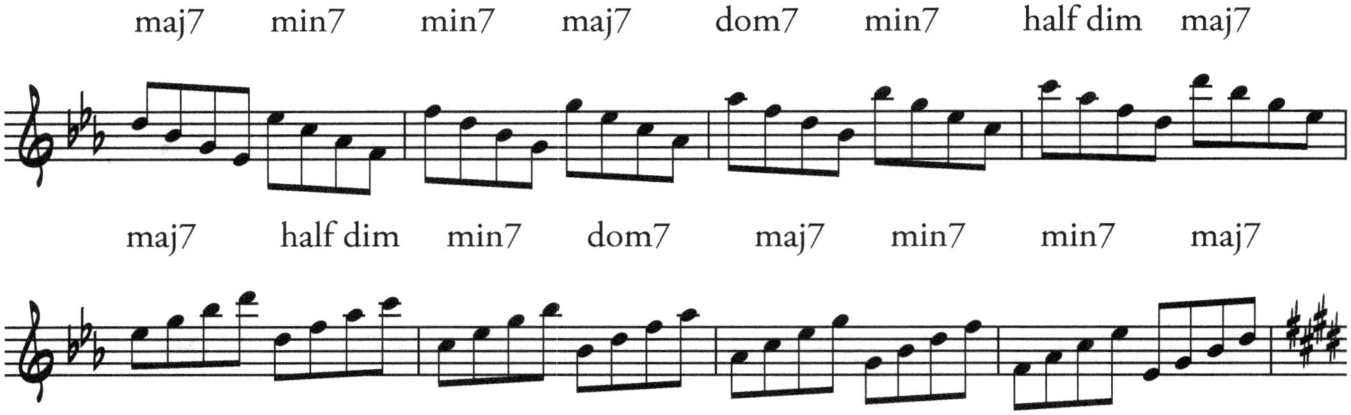

Scale studies in the key of E Major

Scales, Modes and Arpeggios over 2 octaves

E Major scale

E maj 7 arpeggio

F# Dorian scale

F# min 7 arpeggio

G# Phrygian scale

G# min 7 arpeggio

A Lydian scale

Amaj 7 arpeggio

B Mixolydian scale

B 7 arpeggio

C# Aeolian scale

C# min7 arpeggio

D# Locrian scale

D# min7 b5 arpeggio

4 Note Scale Groupings

The following exercise outlines the use of 4 note groupings moving stepwise diatonically through the scale of E major.

For example, the 4 note grouping starts on the root note or 1st degree of the scale and progresses stepwise. The exercise then descends from the 2nd octave E back to the root.

Ascending

Descending

Permutation 2

Up & Down

As in the previous exercise the following exercise outlines the use of 4 note groupings moving stepwise diatonically through the scale of E major.

Notice in exercise #2 the 4 note grouping starts on the root note or 1st degree of the scale and progresses stepwise. In this example we descend when we hit the 5th note in the sequence eg. descending from the 2nd 4 note grouping.

Ascending

Descending

Broken Thirds

Ascending

Descending

3 Note Groupings

E major scale in triplet groupings
Ascending

Descending

Diatonic 7th Chords in Triplets

E maj arpeggio

F# min7 arpeggio

G# min7 arpeggio

A maj 7 arpeggio

B 7 arpeggio

C# min7 arpeggio

D# min7 b5 arpeggio

E maj arpeggio

4 Note Groupings Diatonic Triads

Ascending 1351

maj min min maj maj min dim maj

Descending 1351

maj dim min maj maj min min maj

Ascending 1531

maj min min maj maj min dim maj

Descending 1531

maj dim min maj maj min min maj

4 Note Groupings Diatonic 7th Chords

Ascending

Descending

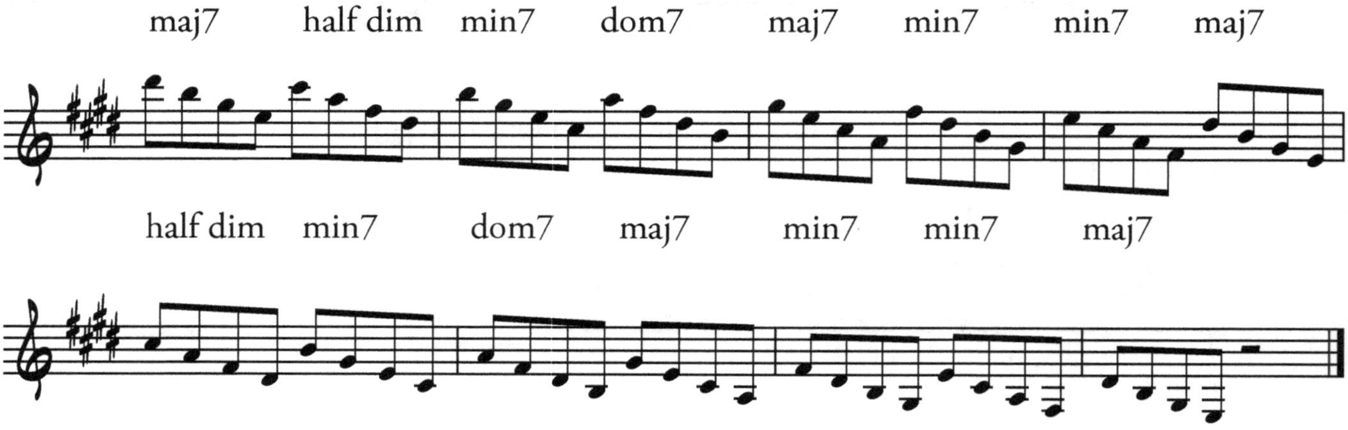

Ascending & descending

Permutation 3

Down the chord stepwise up the scale

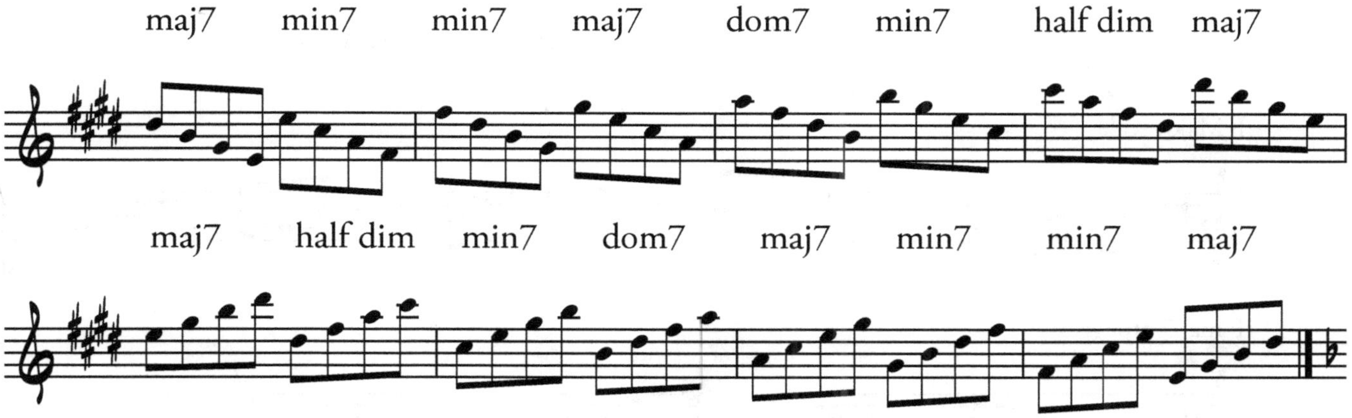

Scale studies in the key of F Major

Scales, Modes and Arpeggios over 2 octaves

F Major scale

F maj 7 arpeggio

G Dorian scale

G min 7 arpeggio

A Phrygian scale

A min 7 arpeggio

Bb Lydian scale

Bb maj 7 arpeggio

C Mixolydian scale

C 7 arpeggio

D Aeolian scale

D min7 arpeggio

E Locrian scale

E min7 b5 arpeggio

4 Note Scale Groupings

The following exercise outlines the use of 4 note groupings moving stepwise diatonically through the scale of F major.

For example, the 4 note grouping starts on the root note or 1st degree of the scale and progresses stepwise. The exercise then descends from the 2nd octave F back to the root.

Ascending

Descending

Permutation 2

Up & Down

As in the previous exercise the following exercise outlines the use of 4 note groupings moving stepwise diatonically through the scale of F major.

Notice in exercise #2 the 4 note grouping starts on the root note or 1st degree of the scale and progresses stepwise. In this example we descend when we hit the 5th note in the sequence eg. descending from the 2nd 4 note grouping.

Ascending

Descending

Broken Thirds

Ascending

Descending

3 Note Groupings

F major scale in triplet groupings
Ascending

Descending

Diatonic 7th Chords in Triplets

F maj arpeggio

G min7 arpeggio

A min7 arpeggio

Bb maj 7 arpeggio

C 7 arpeggio

D min7 arpeggio

E min7 b5 arpeggio

F major arpeggio

4 Note Groupings Diatonic Triads

Ascending 1351

maj min min maj maj min dim maj

Descending 1351

maj dim min maj maj min min maj

Ascending 1531

maj min min maj maj min dim maj

Descending 1531

maj dim min maj maj min min maj

4 Note Groupings Diatonic 7th Chords

Ascending

Descending

Permutation 2

Ascending & descending

Permutation 3
Down the chord stepwise up the scale

Scale studies in the key of F# Major

Scales, Modes and Arpeggios over 2 octaves

F# Major scale

F# maj 7 arpeggio

G# Dorian scale

G# min 7 arpeggio

A# Phrygian scale

A# min 7 arpeggio

B Lydian scale

B major 7 arpeggio

C# Mixolydian scale

C# 7 arpeggio

D# Aeolian scale

D# min7 arpeggio

E# Locrian scale

E# min7 b5 arpeggio

4 Note Scale Groupings

The following exercise outlines the use of 4 note groupings moving stepwise diatonically through the scale of F# major.
For example, the 4 note grouping starts on the root note or 1st degree of the scale and progresses stepwise. The exercise then descends from the 2nd octave F# back to the root.

Ascending

Descending

Permutation 2

Up & Down

As in the previous exercise the following exercise outlines the use of 4 note groupings moving stepwise diatonically through the scale of F# major.

Notice in exercise #2 the 4 note grouping starts on the root note or 1st degree of the scale and progresses stepwise. In this example we descend when we hit the 5th note in the sequence eg. descending from the 2nd 4 note grouping.

Ascending

Descending

Broken Thirds

Ascending

Descending

3 Note Groupings

F# major scale in triplet groupings

Ascending

Descending

Diatonic 7th Chords in Ttriplets

F# maj arpeggio

G# min7 arpeggio

A# min7 arpeggio

B maj 7 arpeggio

C# 7 arpeggio

D# min7 arpeggio

E# min7 b5 arpeggio

F# maj arpeggio

4 Note Groupings Diatonic Triads

Ascending 1351

maj min min maj maj min dim maj

Descending 1351

maj dim min maj maj min min maj

Ascending 1531

maj min min maj maj min dim maj

Descending 1531

maj dim min maj maj min min maj

4 Note Groupings Diatonic 7th Chords

Ascending

maj7 min7 min7 maj7 dom7 min7 half dim maj7

min7 min7 maj7 dom7 min7 half dim maj7

Descending

maj7 half dim min7 dom7 maj7 min7 min7 maj7

half dim min7 dom7 maj7 min7 min7 maj7

Permutation 2
Ascending & descending

maj7 min7 min7 maj7 dom7 min7 half dim maj7

half dim min7 dom7 maj7 min7 min7 maj7

Permutation 3
Down the chord stepwise up the scale

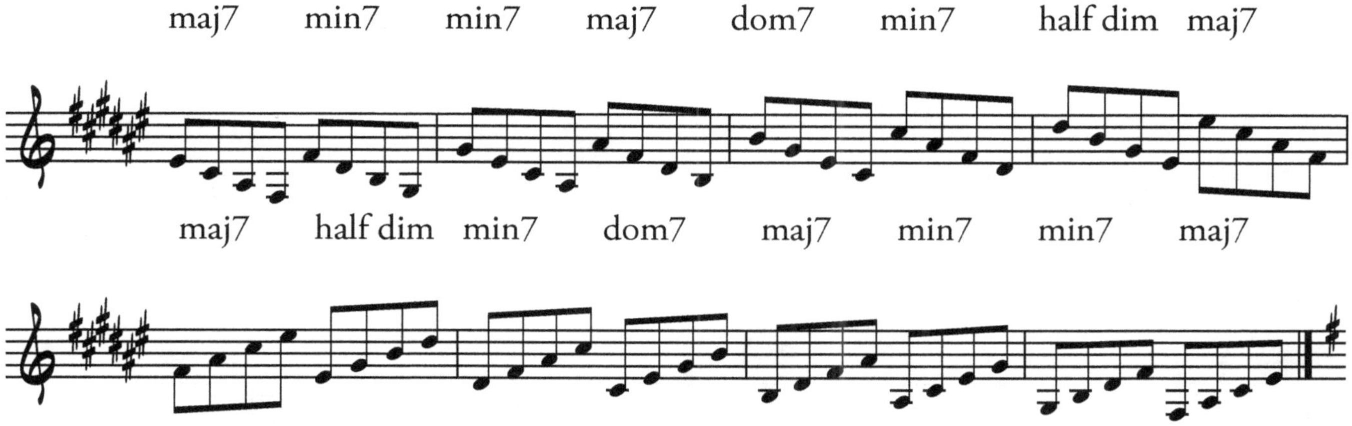

Scale studies in the key of G Major

Scales, Modes and Arpeggios over 2 octaves

G Major scale

G maj 7 arpeggio

A Dorian scale

A min 7 arpeggio

B Phrygian scale

B min 7 arpeggio

C Lydian scale

C maj 7 arpeggio

D Mixolydian scale

D 7 arpeggio

E Aeolian scale

E min7 arpeggio

F# Locrian scale

F# min7 b5 arpeggio

4 Note Scale Groupings

The following exercise outlines the use of 4 note groupings moving stepwise diatonically through the scale of G major.

For example, the 4 note grouping starts on the root note or 1st degree of the scale and progresses stepwise. The exercise then descends from the 2nd octave G back to the root.

Ascending

Descending

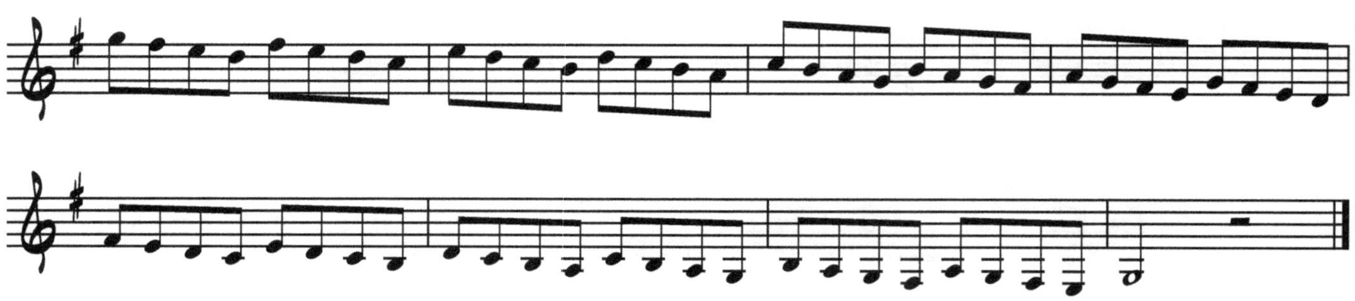

Permutation 2

Up & Down

As in the previous exercise the following exercise outlines the use of 4 note groupings moving stepwise diatonically through the scale of G major.

Notice in exercise #2 the 4 note grouping starts on the root note or 1st degree of the scale and progresses stepwise. In this example we descend when we hit the 5th note in the sequence eg. descending from the 2nd 4 note grouping.

Ascending

Descending

Broken Thirds

Ascending

Descending

3 Note Groupings

G major scale in triplet groupings
Ascending

Descending

Diatonic 7th Chords in Triplets

G Maj arpeggio

A min7 arpeggio

B min7 arpeggio

C maj 7 arpeggio

D 7 arpeggio

E min7 arpeggio

F# min7 b5 arpeggio

G major arpeggio

4 Note Groupings Diatonic Triads

Ascending 1351

Descending 1351

Ascending 1531

Descending 1531

4 Note Groupings Diatonic 7th Chords

Ascending

Descending

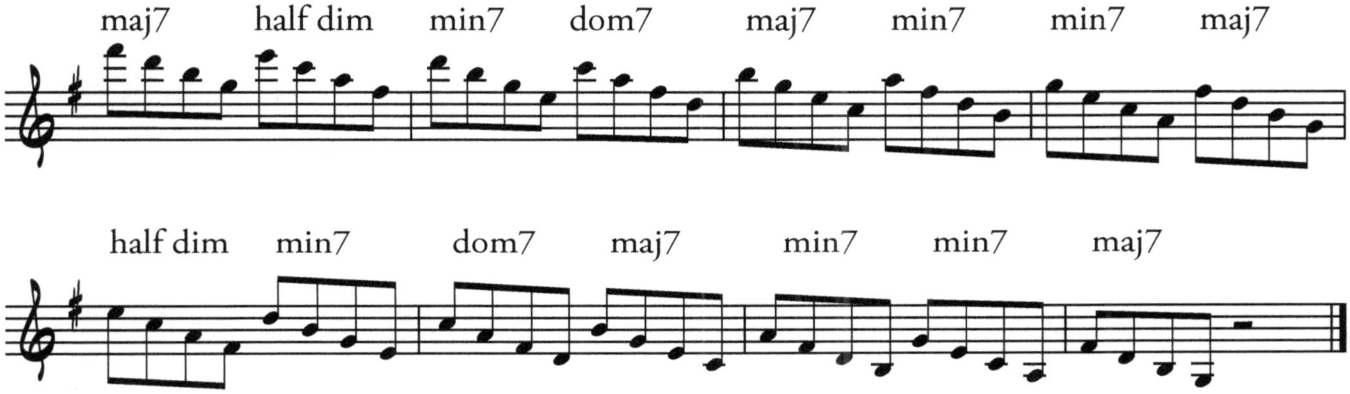

Permutation 2
Ascending & descending

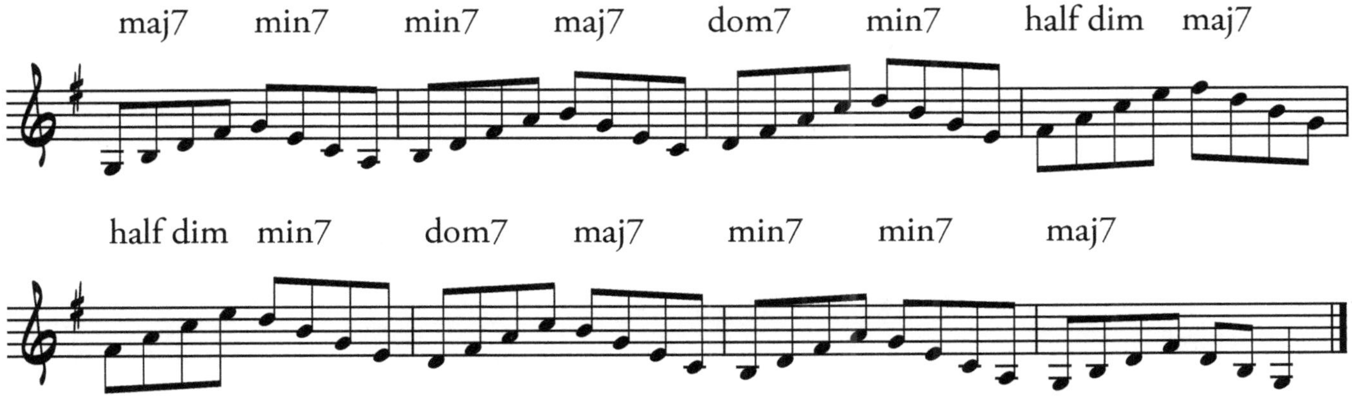

Permutation 3
Down the chord stepwise up the scale

Scale studies in the key of Ab Major

Scales, Modes and Arpeggios over 2 octaves

Ab Major scale

Ab maj 7 arpeggio

Bb Dorian scale

Bb min 7 arpeggio

C Phrygian scale

C min 7 arpeggio

Db Lydian scale

Db maj 7 arpeggio

Eb Mixolydian scale

Eb 7 arpeggio

F Aeolian scale

F min7 arpeggio

G Locrian scale

G min7 b5 arpeggio

4 Note Scale Groupings

The following exercise outlines the use of 4 note groupings moving stepwise diatonically through the scale of Ab major.

For example, the 4 note grouping starts on the root note or 1st degree of the scale and progresses stepwise. The exercise then descends from the 2nd octave Ab back to the root.

Ascending

Descending

Permutation 2

Up & Down

As in the previous exercise the following exercise outlines the use of 4 note groupings moving stepwise diatonically through the scale of Ab major.

Notice in exercise #2 the 4 note grouping starts on the root note or 1st degree of the scale and progresses stepwise. In this example we descend when we hit the 5th note in the sequence eg. descending from the 2nd 4 note grouping.

Ascending

Descending

Broken Thirds

Ascending

Descending

3 Note Groupings

Ab major scale in triplet groupings

Ascending

Descending

Diatonic 7th Chords in Triplets

Ab maj arpeggio

Bb min7 arpeggio

C min7 arpeggio

Db maj 7 arpeggio

Eb 7 arpeggio

F min7 arpeggio

G min7 b5 arpeggio

Ab maj arpeggio

4 Note Groupings Diatonic Triads

Ascending 1351

Descending 1351

Ascending 1531

Descending 1531

4 Note Groupings Diatonic 7th Chords

Ascending

Descending

Permutation 2
Ascending & descending

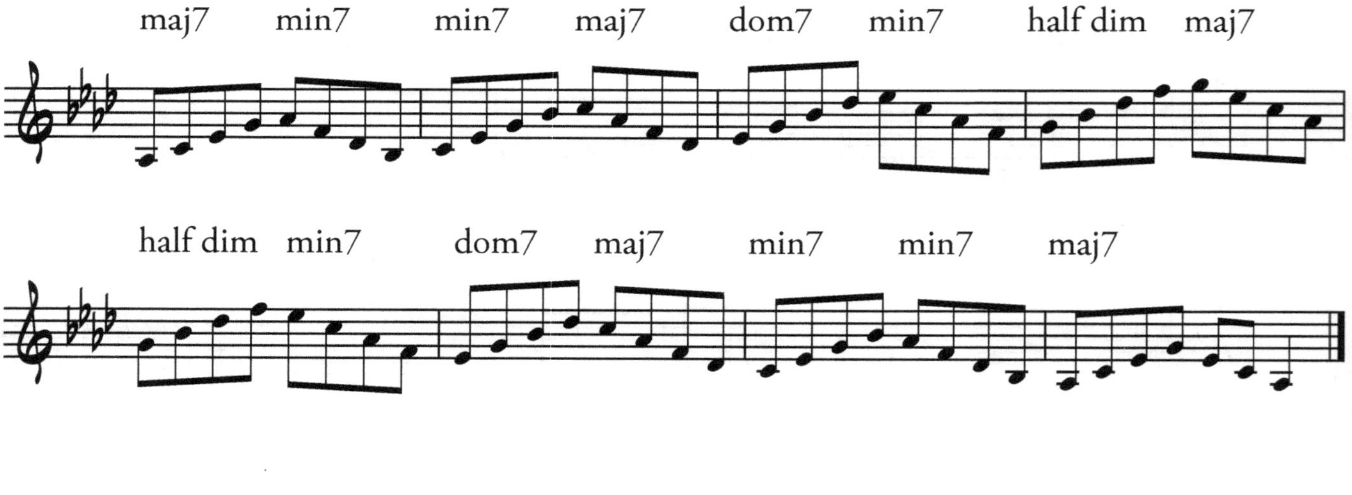

Permutation 3

Down the chord stepwise up the scale

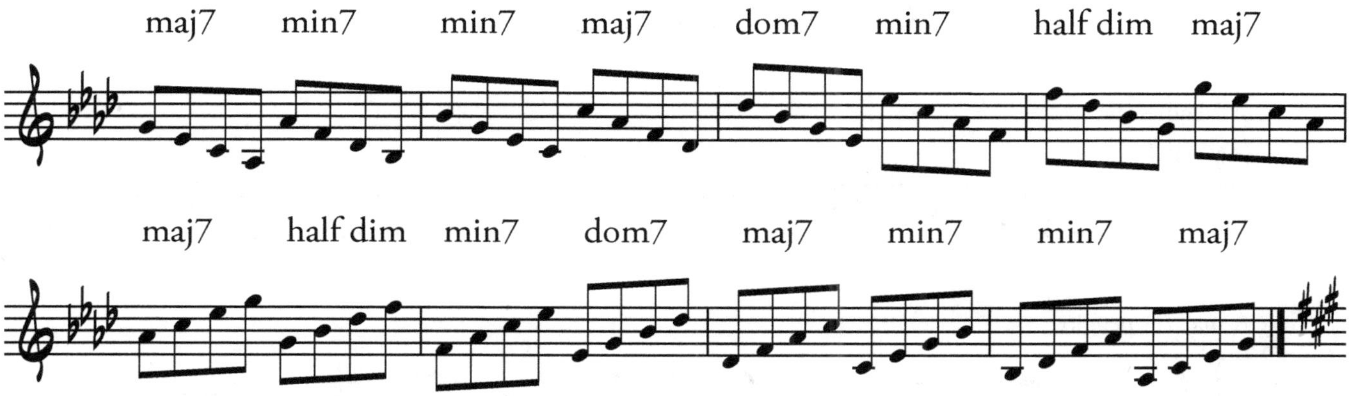

Scale studies in the key of A Major

Scales, Modes and Arpeggios over 2 octaves

A Major scale

A maj 7 arpeggio

B Dorian scale

B min 7 arpeggio

C# Phrygian scale

C# min 7 arpeggio

D Lydian scale

D maj 7 arpeggio

E Mixolydian scale

E 7 arpeggio

F# Aeolian scale

F# min7 arpeggio

G# Locrian scale

G# min7 b5 arpeggio

4 Note Scale Groupings

The following exercise outlines the use of 4 note groupings moving stepwise diatonically through the scale of A major.

For example, the 4 note grouping starts on the root note or 1st degree of the scale and progresses stepwise. The exercise then descends from the 2nd octave A back to the root.

Ascending

Descending

Permutation 2

Up & Down

As in the previous exercise the following exercise outlines the use of 4 note groupings moving stepwise diatonically through the scale of A major.

Notice in exercise #2 the 4 note grouping starts on the root note or 1st degree of the scale and progresses stepwise. In this example we descend when we hit the 5th note in the sequence eg. descending from the 2nd 4 note grouping.

Ascending

Descending

Broken Thirds

Ascending

Descending

3 Note Groupings

A major scale in triplet groupings
Ascending

Descending

Diatonic 7th Chords in Triplets

A maj arpeggio

B min7 arpeggio

C# min7 arpeggio

D maj 7 arpeggio

E 7 arpeggio

F# min7 arpeggio

G# min7 b5 arpeggio

A maj arpeggio

4 Note Groupings Diatonic Triads

Ascending 1351

Descending 1351

Ascending 1531

Descending 1531

4 Note Groupings Diatonic 7th Chords

Ascending

Descending

Permutation 2
Ascending & descending

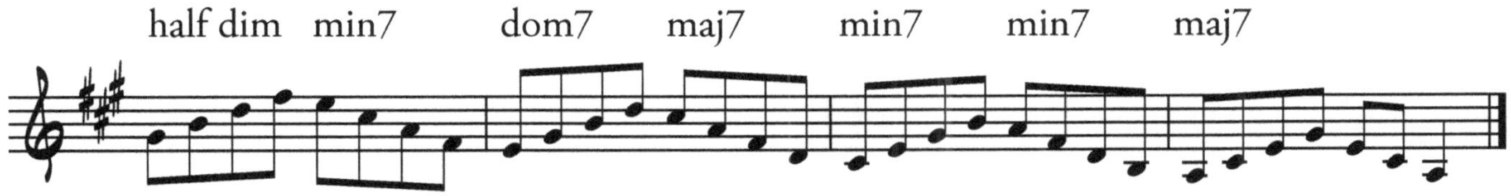

Permutation 3

Down the chord stepwise up the scale

Scale studies in the key of Bb Major

Scales, Modes and Arpeggios over 2 octaves

Bb Major scale

Bb maj 7 arpeggio

C Dorian scale

C min 7 arpeggio

D Phrygian scale

D min 7 arpeggio

Eb Lydian scale

Eb maj 7 arpeggio

F Mixolydian scale

F 7 arpeggio

G Aeolian scale

G min7 arpeggio

A Locrian scale

A min7 b5 arpeggio

4 Note Scale Groupings

The following exercise outlines the use of 4 note groupings moving stepwise diatonically through the scale of Bb major.

For example, the 4 note grouping starts on the root note or 1st degree of the scale and progresses stepwise. The exercise then descends from the 2nd octave Bb back to the root.

Ascending

Descending

Permutation 2

Up & Down

As in the previous exercise the following exercise outlines the use of 4 note groupings moving stepwise diatonically through the scale of Bb major.

Notice in exercise #2 the 4 note grouping starts on the root note or 1st degree of the scale and progresses stepwise. In this example we descend when we hit the 5th note in the sequence eg. descending from the 2nd 4 note grouping.

Ascending

Descending

Broken Thirds

Ascending

Descending

3 Note Groupings

Bb major scale in triplet groupings
Ascending

Descending

Diatonic 7th Chords in Triplets

Bb maj arpeggio

C min7 arpeggio

D min7 arpeggio

Eb maj 7 arpeggio

F 7 arpeggio

G min7 arpeggio

A min7 b5 arpeggio

Bb major arpeggio

4 Note Groupings Diatonic Triads

Ascending 1351

Descending 1351

Ascending 1531

Descending 1531

4 Note Groupings Diatonic 7th Chords

Ascending

Descending

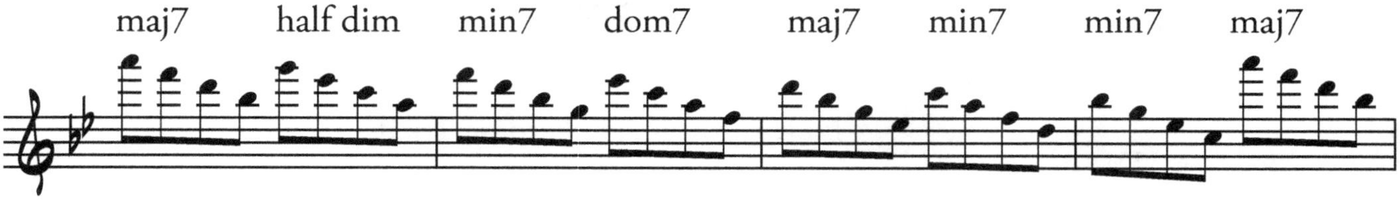

Permutation 2

Ascending & descending

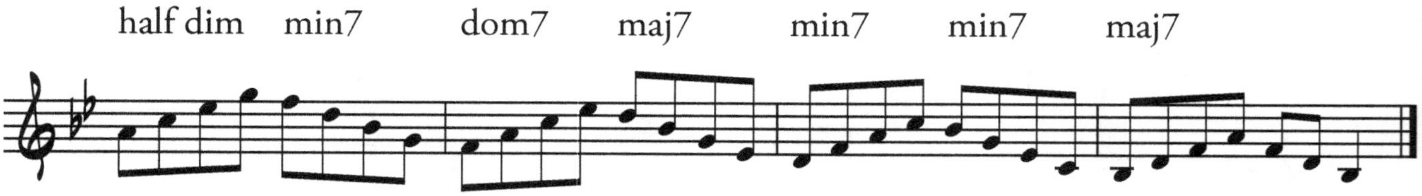

Permutation 3
Down the chord stepwise up the scale

Scale studies in the key of B Major

Scales, Modes and Arpeggios over 2 octaves

B Major scale

B maj 7 arpeggio

C# Dorian scale

C# min 7 arpeggio

D# Phrygian scale

D# min 7 arpeggio

E Lydian scale

E maj 7 arpeggio

F# Mixolydian scale

F# 7 arpeggio

G# Aeolian scale

G# min7 arpeggio

A# Locrian scale

A# min7 b5 arpeggio

4 Note Scale Groupings

The following exercise outlines the use of 4 note groupings moving stepwise diatonically through the scale of B major.
For example, the 4 note grouping starts on the root note or 1st degree of the scale and progresses stepwise. The exercise then descends from the 2nd octave B back to the root.

Ascending

Descending

Permutation 2

Up & Down

As in the previous exercise the following exercise outlines the use of 4 note groupings moving stepwise diatonically through the scale of B major.

Notice in exercise #2 the 4 note grouping starts on the root note or 1st degree of the scale and progresses stepwise. In this example we descend when we hit the 5th note in the sequence eg. descending from the 2nd 4 note grouping.

Ascending

Descending

Broken Thirds

Ascending

Descending

3 Note Groupings

B major scale in triplet groupings
Ascending

Descending

Diatonic 7th Chords in Triplets

B maj arpeggio

C# min7 arpeggio

D# min7 arpeggio

E maj 7 arpeggio

F# 7 arpeggio

G# min7 arpeggio

A# min7 b5 arpeggio

B maj arpeggio

4 Note Groupings Diatonic Triads

Ascending 1351

Descending 1351

Ascending 1531

Descending 1531

4 Note Groupings Diatonic 7th Chords

Ascending

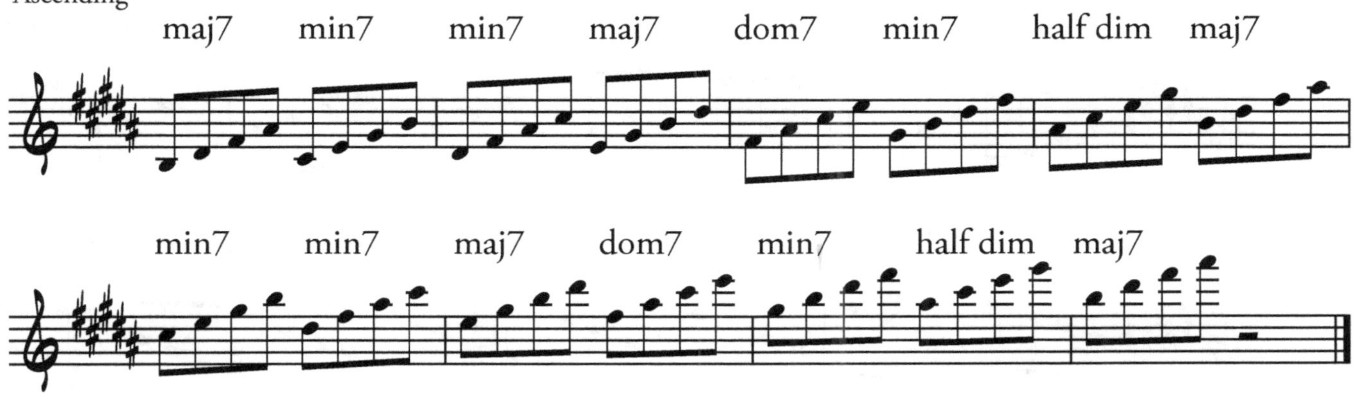

Descending

Permutation 2
Ascending & descending

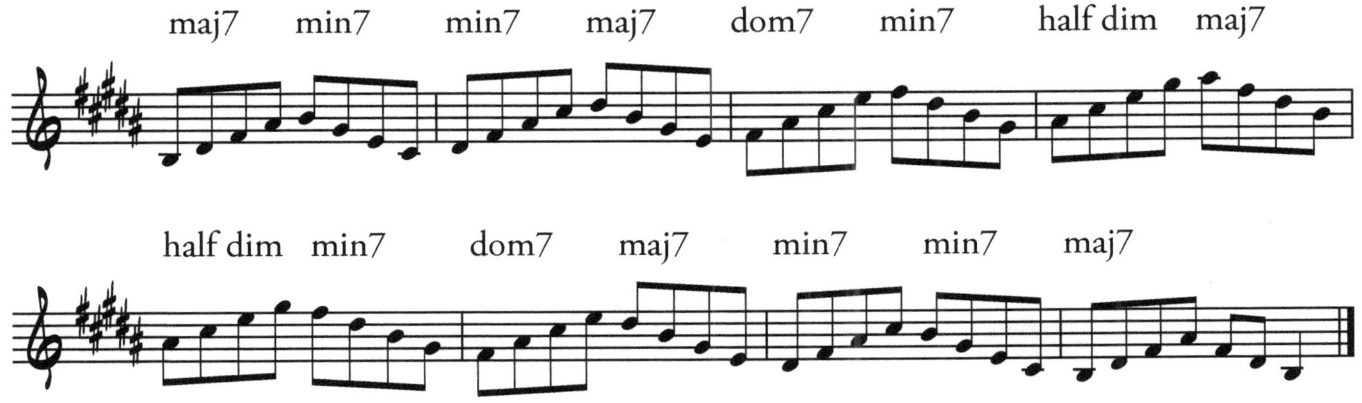

Permutation 3

Down the chord stepwise up the scale

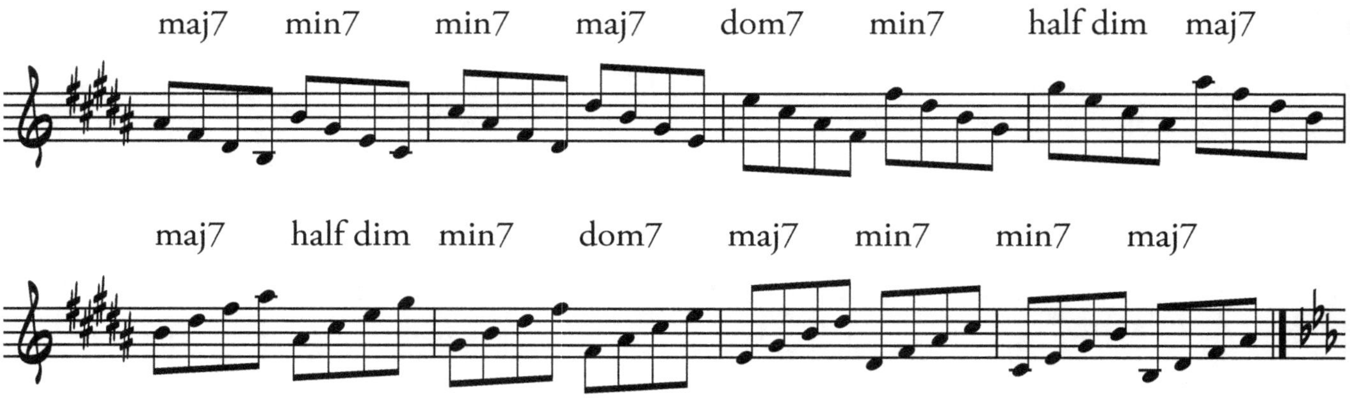

Part 2. Scale studies in the key of C Melodic Minor (Ascending)*

Scales, Modes and Arpeggios over 2 octaves

C Melodic minor scale

C min maj7 arpeggio

D sus b9 scale

D min7 arpeggio * *

Eb Lydian augmented scale

Eb maj #5 arpeggio

F Lydian dominant scale

F 7 #11 arpeggio

* For the purpose of this book we will be using the ascending melodic minor scale also known as the " jazz minor scale ". The melodic minor scale uses a different interval structure when descending when used in classical music.

** Shown here are the " diatonic " 7th chords built from the scale eg min 7th and not a Sus b9 arpeggio.

C Melodic minor/G scale

G7 arpeggio

A Locrian #2 scale

A min7 b5 arpeggio

B Altered scale

B Alt. arpeggio

4 Note Scale Groupings

The following exercise outlines the use of 4 note groupings moving stepwise diatonically through the scale of C melodic minor

For example, the 4 note grouping starts on the root note or 1st degree of the scale and progresses stepwise. The exercise then descends from the 2nd octave C back to the root.

Ascending

Descending

Permutation 2

Up & Down

As in the previous exercise the following exercise outlines the use of 4 note groupings moving stepwise diatonically through the scale of C melodic minor.

Notice in exercise #2 the 4 note grouping starts on the root note or 1st degree of the scale and progresses stepwise. In this example we descend when we hit the 5th note in the sequence eg. descending from the 2nd 4 note grouping.

Ascending

Descending

Broken Thirds

Ascending

Descending

3 Note Groupings

C Melodic minor scale in triplet groupings
Ascending

Descending

Diatonic 7th Chords in Triplets

Starting on the Root
C min/maj7 arpeggio

Starting on the 2nd
D min7 arpeggio

Starting on the 3rd
Eb maj7/#5 arpeggio

Starting on the 4th
F 7#11 arpeggio

Starting on the 5th
G7 arpeggio

Starting on the 6th
A min7b5 arpeggio

Starting on the 7th
B min7 b5 arpeggio

Starting on the Root
C min/maj7 arpeggio

4 Note Groupings Diatonic Triads

Ascending 1351

Descending 1351

Ascending 1531

Descending 1531

4 Note Groupings Diatonic 7th Chords

Ascending

Descending

Permutation 2
Ascending & descending

Permutation 3
Down the chord stepwise up the scale

Scale studies in the key of C# Melodic Minor

Scales, Modes and Arpeggios over 2 octaves

C# Melodic minor scale

C# min maj7 arpeggio

D# sus b9 scale

D# sus b9 arpeggio

E Lydian augmented scale

E maj #5 arpeggio

F# Lydian dominant scale

F# 7 #11 arpeggio

C# Melodic minor/G# scale

C# minmaj7 /G# arpeggio

A# Locrian #2 scale

A# min7 b5 arpeggio

B# Altered scale

B# Alt. arpeggio

4 Note Scale Groupings

The following exercise outlines the use of 4 note groupings moving stepwise diatonically through the scale of C# melodic minor.

For example, the 4 note grouping starts on the root note or 1st degree of the scale and progresses stepwise . The exercise then descends from the 2nd octave C# back to the root.

Ascending

Descending

Permutation 2 Up & Down

As in the previous exercise the following exercise outlines the use of 4 note groupings moving stepwise diatonically through the scale of C# melodic minor.

Notice in exercise #2 the 4 note grouping starts on the root note or 1st degree of the scale and progresses stepwise. In this example we descend when we hit the 5th note in the sequence eg. descending from the 2nd 4 note grouping.

Ascending

Descending

Broken Thirds

Ascending

Descending

3 Note Groupings

C # Melodic minor scale in triplet groupings
Ascending

Descending

Diatonic 7th Chords in Triplets

Starting on the Root
C# min/maj7 arpeggio

Starting on the 2nd
D# min7 arpeggio

Starting on the 3rd
E maj7/#5 arpeggio

Starting on the 4th
F# 7#11 arpeggio

Starting on the 5th
G# 7 arpeggio

Starting on the 6th
A# min7b5 arpeggio

Starting on the 7th
B# min7 b5 arpeggio

Starting on the Root
C# min/maj7 arpeggio

4 Note Groupings Diatonic Triads

Ascending 1351

min min aug maj maj dim dim min

Descending 1351

min dim dim maj maj aug min min

Ascending 1531

min min aug maj maj dim dim min

Descending 1531

min dim dim maj maj aug min min

4 Note Groupings Diatonic 7th Chords

Ascending

Descending

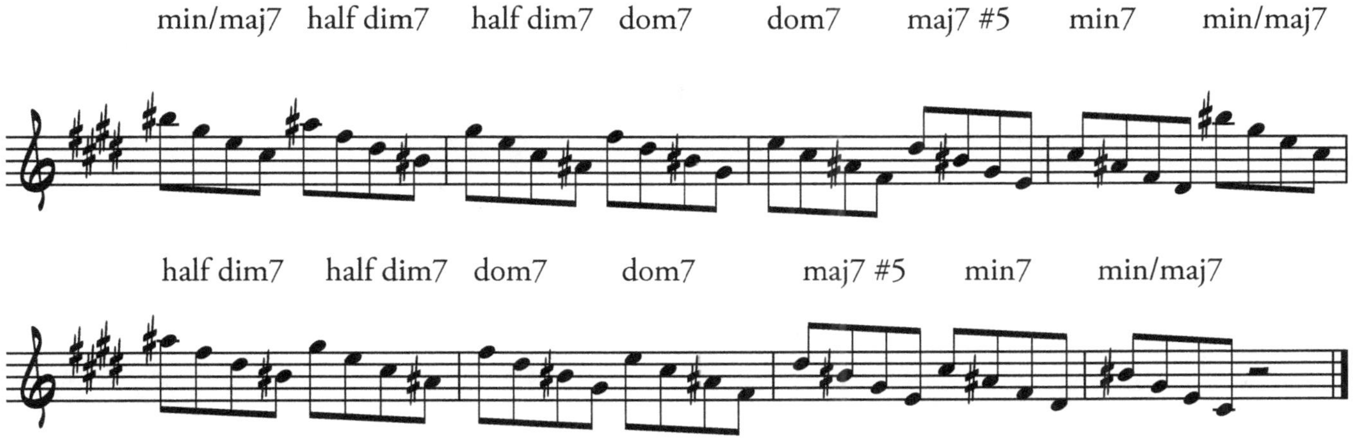

Permutation 2
Ascending & descending

Permutation 3

Down the chord stepwise up the scale

Scale studies in the key of D Melodic Minor

Scales, Modes and Arpeggios over 2 octaves

D Melodic minor scale

D min maj7 arpeggio

E sus b9 scale

E sus b9 arpeggio

F Lydian augmented scale

F maj #5 arpeggio

G Lydian dominant scale

G 7 #11 arpeggio

D Melodic minor/A scale

D minmaj7 /A arpeggio

B Locrian #2 scale

B min7 b5 arpeggio

C# Altered scale

C# Alt. arpeggio

4 Note Scale Groupings

The following exercise outlines the use of 4 note groupings moving stepwise diatonically through the scale of D melodic minor.

For example, the 4 note grouping starts on the root note or 1st degree of the scale and progresses stepwise . The exercise then descends from the 2nd octave D back to the root.

Ascending

Descending

Permutation 2 Up & Down

As in the previous exercise the following exercise outlines the use of 4 note groupings moving stepwise diatonically through the scale of D melodic minor.

Notice in exercise #2 the 4 note grouping starts on the root note or 1st degree of the scale and progresses stepwise. In this example we descend when we hit the 5th note in the sequence eg. descending from the 2nd 4 note grouping.

Ascending

Descending

Broken Thirds

Ascending

Descending

3 Note Groupings

D Melodic minor scale in triplet groupings
Ascending

Descending

Diatonic 7th Chords in Triplets

Starting on the Root
D min/maj7 arpeggio

Starting on the 2nd
E min7 arpeggio

Starting on the 3rd
F maj7/#5 arpeggio

Starting on the 4th
G 7#11 arpeggio

Starting on the 5th
A7 arpeggio

Starting on the 6th
B min7 b5 arpeggio

Starting on the 7th
C# min7 b5 arpeggio

Starting on the Root
D min/maj 7 arpeggio

4 Note Grouping Diatonic Triads

Ascending 1351

Descending 1351

Ascending 1531

Descending 1531

4 Note Groupings Diatonic 7th Chords

Ascending

min/maj7 min7 maj7#5 dom7 dom7 half dim7 half dim7 min/maj7

min7 maj7#5 dom7 dom7 half dim7 half dim7 min/maj7

Descending

min/maj7 half dim7 half dim7 dom7 dom7 maj7 #5 min7 min/maj7

half dim7 half dim7 dom7 dom7 maj7 #5 min7 min/maj7

Permutation 2
Ascending & descending

min/maj7 min7 maj7#5 dom7 dom7 half dim7 half dim7 min/maj7

half dim7 half dim7 dom7 dom7 maj7#5 min7 min/maj7

Permutation 3
Down the chord stepwise up the scale

Scale studies in the key of Eb Melodic Minor

Scales, Modes and Arpeggios over 2 octaves

Eb Melodic minor scale

Eb min maj7 arpeggio

F sus b9 scale

F sus b9 arpeggio

Gb Lydian augmented scale

Gb maj #5 arpeggio

Ab Lydian dominant scale

Ab7 #11 arpeggio

Eb Melodic minor/Bb scale

Eb minmaj7 /Bb arpeggio

C Locrian #2 scale

C min7 b5 arpeggio

D Altered scale

D Alt. arpeggio

4 Note Scale Groupings

The following exercise outlines the use of 4 note groupings moving stepwise diatonically through the scale of Eb melodic minor.

For example, the 4 note grouping starts on the root note or 1st degree of the scale and progresses stepwise . The exercise then descends from the 2nd octave Eb back to the root.

Ascending

Descending

Permutation 2 Up & Down

As in the previous exercise the following exercise outlines the use of 4 note groupings moving stepwise diatonically through the scale of Eb melodic minor.

Notice in exercise #2 the 4 note grouping starts on the root note or 1st degree of the scale and progresses stepwise. In this example we descend when we hit the 5th note in the sequence eg. descending from the 2nd 4 note grouping.

Ascending

Descending

Broken Thirds

Ascending

Descending

3 Note Groupings

Eb Melodic minor scale in triplet groupings
Ascending

Descending

Diatonic 7th Chords in Triplets

Starting on the Root
Eb min/maj7 arpeggio

Starting on the 2nd
F min7 arpeggio

Starting on the 3rd
Gb maj7/#5 arpeggio

Starting on the 4th
Ab 7#11 arpeggio

Starting on the 5th
Bb7 arpeggio

Starting on the 6th
C min7 b5 arpeggio

Starting on the 7th
D min7 b5 arpeggio

Starting on the Root
Eb min/maj 7 arpeggio

4 Note Groupings Diatonic Triads

Ascending 1351

Descending 1351

Ascending 1531

Descending 1531

4 Note Groupings Diatonic 7th Chords

Ascending

Descending

Permutation 2
Ascending & descending

Permutation 3

Down the chord stepwise up the scale

Scale studies in the key of E Melodic Minor

Scales, Modes and Arpeggios over 2 octaves

E Melodic minor scale

E min maj 7 arpeggio

F# sus b9 scale

F# sus b9 arpeggio

G Lydian augmented scale

G maj #5 arpeggio

A Lydian dominant scale

A 7 #11 arpeggio

E Melodic minor/B scale

E minmaj7 / B arpeggio

C# Locrian #2 scale

C# min7 b5 arpeggio

D# Altered scale

D# Alt. arpeggio

4 Note Scale Groupings

The following exercise outlines the use of 4 note groupings moving stepwise diatonically through the scale of E melodic minor.

For example, the 4 note grouping starts on the root note or 1st degree of the scale and progresses stepwise . The exercise then descends from the 2nd octave E back to the root.

Ascending

Descending

Permutation 2 — Up & Down

As in the previous exercise the following exercise outlines the use of 4 note groupings moving stepwise diatonically through the scale of E melodic minor.
Notice in exercise #2 the 4 note grouping starts on the root note or 1st degree of the scale and progresses stepwise. In this example we descend when we hit the 5th note in the sequence eg. descending from the 2nd 4 note grouping.

Ascending

Descending

Broken Thirds

Ascending

Descending

3 Note Groupings

E Melodic minor scale in triplet groupings
Ascending

Descending

Diatonic 7th Chords in Triplets

Starting on the Root
E min/maj7 arpeggio

Starting on the 2nd
F# min7 arpeggio

Starting on the 3rd
G maj7/#5 arpeggio

Starting on the 4th
A 7#11 arpeggio

Starting on the 5th
B 7 arpeggio

Starting on the 6th
C# min7 b5 arpeggio

Starting on the 7th
D# min7 b5 arpeggio

Starting on the Root
E min/maj 7 arpeggio

4 Note Groupings Diatonic Triads

Ascending 1351

Descending 1351

Ascending 1531

Descending 1531

4 Note Groupings Diatonic 7th Chords

Ascending

Descending

Permutation 2
Ascending & descending

Permutation 3

Down the chord stepwise up the scale

Scale studies in the key of F Melodic Minor

Scales, Modes and Arpeggios over 2 octaves

F Melodic minor scale

F min maj7 arpeggio

G sus b9 scale

G sus b9 arpeggio

Ab Lydian augmented scale

Ab maj #5 arpeggio

Bb Lydian dominant scale

Bb 7 #11 arpeggio

F Melodic minor/ C scale

F minmaj7 / C arpeggio

D Locrian #2 scale

D min7 b5 arpeggio

E Altered scale

E Alt. arpeggio

4 Note Scale Groupings

The following exercise outlines the use of 4 note groupings moving stepwise diatonically through the scale of F melodic minor.

For example, the 4 note grouping starts on the root note or 1st degree of the scale and progresses stepwise . The exercise then descends from the 2nd octave F back to the root.

Ascending

Descending

Permutation 2 Up & Down

As in the previous exercise the following exercise outlines the use of 4 note groupings moving stepwise diatonically through the scale of F melodic minor.

Notice in exercise #2 the 4 note grouping starts on the root note or 1st degree of the scale and progresses stepwise. In this example we descend when we hit the 5th note in the sequence eg. descending from the 2nd 4 note grouping.

Ascending

Descending

Broken Thirds

Ascending

Descending

3 Note Groupings

F Melodic minor scale in triplet groupings
Ascending

Descending

Diatonic 7th Chords in Triplets

Starting on the Root
F min/maj7 arpeggio

Starting on the 2nd
G min7 arpeggio

Starting on the 3rd
Ab maj7/#5 arpeggio

Starting on the 4th
Bb 7#11 arpeggio

Starting on the 5th
C 7 arpeggio

Starting on the 6th
D min7 b5 arpeggio

Starting on the 7th
E min7 b5 arpeggio

Starting on the Root
F min/maj 7 arpeggio

4 Note Groupings Diatonic Triads

Ascending 1351

Descending 1351

Ascending 1531

Descending 1531

4 Note Groupings Diatonic 7th Chords

Ascending

min/maj7 min7 maj7#5 dom7 dom7 half dim7 half dim7 min/maj7

min7 maj7#5 dom7 dom7 half dim7 half dim7 min/maj7

Descending

min/maj7 half dim7 half dim7 dom7 dom7 maj7 #5 min7 min/maj7

half dim7 half dim7 dom7 dom7 maj7 #5 min7 min/maj7

Permutation 2
Ascending & descending

min/maj7 min7 maj7#5 dom7 dom7 half dim7 half dim7 min/maj7

half dim7 half dim7 dom7 dom7 maj7#5 min7 min/maj7

Permutation 3

Down the chord stepwise up the scale

Scale studies in the key of F# Melodic Minor

Scales, Modes and Arpeggios over 2 octaves

F# Melodic minor scale

F# min maj7 arpeggio

G# sus b9 scale

G# sus b9 arpeggio

A Lydian augmented scale

A maj #5 arpeggio

B Lydian dominant scale

B 7 #11 arpeggio

F# Melodic minor/ C# scale

F# minmaj7 / C# arpeggio

D# Locrian #2 scale

D# min7 b5 arpeggio

E# Altered scale

E# Alt. arpeggio

4 Note Scale Groupings

The following exercise outlines the use of 4 note groupings moving stepwise diatonically through the scale of F# melodic minor.

For example, the 4 note grouping starts on the root note or 1st degree of the scale and progresses stepwise . The exercise then descends from the 2nd octave F# back to the root.

Ascending

Descending

Permutation 2 — Up & Down

As in the previous exercise the following exercise outlines the use of 4 note groupings moving stepwise diatonically through the scale of F# melodic minor.

Notice in exercise #2 the 4 note grouping starts on the root note or 1st degree of the scale and progresses stepwise. In this example we descend when we hit the 5th note in the sequence eg. descending from the 2nd 4 note grouping.

Ascending

Descending

Broken Thirds

Ascending

Descending

3 Note Groupings

F# Melodic minor scale in triplet groupings
Ascending

Descending

Diatonic 7th Chords in Triplets

Starting on the Root
F# min/maj7 arpeggio

Starting on the 2nd
G# min7 arpeggio

Starting on the 3rd
A maj7/#5 arpeggio

Starting on the 4th
B 7#11 arpeggio

Starting on the 5th
C# 7 arpeggio

Starting on the 6th
D# min7 b5 arpeggio

Starting on the 7th
E# min7 b5 arpeggio

Starting on the Root
F# min/maj 7 arpeggio

4 Note Groupings Diatonic Triads

Ascending 1351

Descending 1351

Ascending 1531

Descending 1531

4 Note Groupings Diatonic 7th Chords

Ascending

min/maj7 min7 maj7#5 dom7 dom7 half dim7 half dim7 min/maj7

min7 maj7#5 dom7 dom7 half dim7 half dim7 min/maj7

Descending

min/maj7 half dim7 half dim7 dom7 dom7 maj7 #5 min7 min/maj7

half dim7 half dim7 dom7 dom7 maj7 #5 min7 min/maj7

Permutation 2
Ascending & descending

min/maj7 min7 maj7#5 dom7 dom7 half dim7 half dim7 min/maj7

half dim7 half dim7 dom7 dom7 maj7#5 min7 min/maj7

Permutation 3
Down the chord stepwise up the scale

Scale studies in the key of G Melodic Minor

Scales, Modes and Arpeggios over 2 octaves

G Melodic minor scale

G min maj7 arpeggio

A sus b9 scale

A sus b9 arpeggio

Bb Lydian augmented scale

Bb maj #5 arpeggio

C Lydian dominant scale

C 7 #11 arpeggio

G Melodic minor/ D scale

G minmaj7 / D arpeggio

E Locrian #2 scale

E min7 b5 arpeggio

F# Altered scale

F# Alt. arpeggio

4 Note Scale Groupings

The following exercise outlines the use of 4 note groupings moving stepwise diatonically through the scale of G melodic minor.

For example, the 4 note grouping starts on the root note or 1st degree of the scale and progresses stepwise . The exercise then descends from the 2nd octave G back to the root.

Ascending

Descending

Permutation 2 Up & Down

As in the previous exercise the following exercise outlines the use of 4 note groupings moving stepwise diatonically through the scale of G melodic minor.

Notice in exercise #2 the 4 note grouping starts on the root note or 1st degree of the scale and progresses stepwise. In this example we descend when we hit the 5th note in the sequence eg. descending from the 2nd 4 note grouping.

Ascending

Descending

Broken Thirds

Ascending

Descending

3 Note Groupings

G Melodic minor scale in triplet groupings
Ascending

Descending

Diatonic 7th Chords in Triplets

Starting on the Root
G min/maj7 arpeggio

Starting on the 2nd
A min7 arpeggio

Starting on the 3rd
Bb maj7/#5 arpeggio

Starting on the 4th
C 7#11 arpeggio

Starting on the 5th
D 7 arpeggio

Starting on the 6th
E min7 b5 arpeggio

Starting on the 7th
F# min7 b5 arpeggio

Starting on the Root
G min/maj 7 arpeggio

4 Note Groupings Diatonic Triads

Ascending 1351

Descending 1351

Ascending 1531

Descending 1531

4 Note Groupings Diatonic 7th Chords

Ascending

min/maj7 min7 maj7#5 dom7 dom7 half dim7 half dim7 min/maj7

min7 maj7#5 dom7 dom7 half dim7 half dim7 min/maj7

Descending

min/maj7 half dim7 half dim7 dom7 dom7 maj7 #5 min7 min/maj7

half dim7 half dim7 dom7 dom7 maj7 #5 min7 min/maj7

Permutation 2

Ascending & descending

min/maj7 min7 maj7#5 dom7 dom7 half dim7 half dim7 min/maj7

half dim7 half dim7 dom7 dom7 maj7#5 min7 min/maj7

Permutation 3

Down the chord stepwise up the scale

Scale studies in the key of Ab Melodic Minor

Scales, Modes and Arpeggios over 2 octaves

Ab Melodic minor scale

Ab min maj7 arpeggio

Bb sus b9 scale

Bb sus b9 arpeggio

Cb Lydian augmented scale

Cb maj #5 arpeggio

Db Lydian dominant scale

Db 7 #11 arpeggio

Ab Melodic minor/ Eb scale

Ab minmaj7 / Eb arpeggio

F Locrian #2 scale

F min7 b5 arpeggio

G Altered scale

G Alt. arpeggio

4 Note Scale Groupings

The following exercise outlines the use of 4 note groupings moving stepwise diatonically through the scale of Ab melodic minor

For example, the 4 note grouping starts on the root note or 1st degree of the scale and progresses stepwise . The exercise then descends from the 2nd octave Ab back to the root.

Ascending

Descending

Permutation 2 Up & Down

As in the previous exercise the following exercise outlines the use of 4 note groupings moving stepwise diatonically through the scale of Ab melodic minor.
Notice in exercise #2 the 4 note grouping starts on the root note or 1st degree of the scale and progresses stepwise. In this example we descend when we hit the 5th note in the sequence eg. descending from the 2nd 4 note grouping.

Ascending

Descending

Broken Thirds

Ascending

Descending

3 Note Groupings

Ab Melodic minor scale in triplet groupings
Ascending

Descending

Diatonic 7th Chords in Triplets

Starting on the Root
Ab min/maj7 arpeggio

Starting on the 2nd
Bb min7 arpeggio

Starting on the 3rd
Cb maj7/#5 arpeggio

Starting on the 4th
Db 7#11 arpeggio

Starting on the 5th
Eb 7 arpeggio

Starting on the 6th
F min7 b5 arpeggio

Starting on the 7th
G min7 b5 arpeggio

Starting on the Root
Ab min/maj 7 arpeggio

4 Note Groupings Diatonic Triads

Ascending 1351

Descending 1351

Ascending 1531

Descending 1531

4 Note Groupings Diatonic 7th Chords

Ascending

Descending

Permutation 2
Ascending & descending

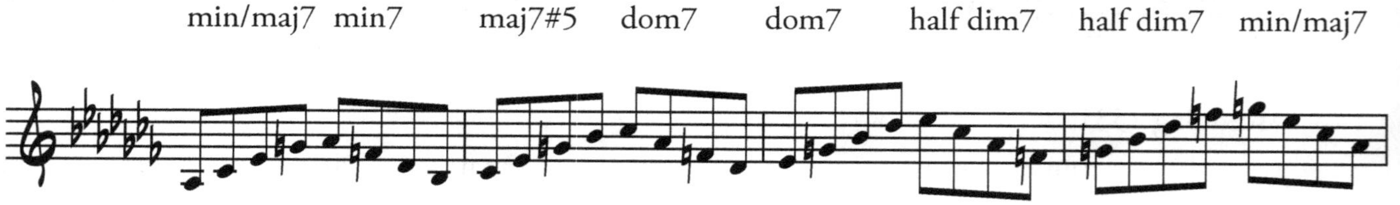

Permutation 3

Down the chord stepwise up the scale

Scale studies in the key of A Melodic Minor

Scales, Modes and Arpeggios over 2 octaves

A Melodic minor scale

A min maj7 arpeggio

B sus b9 scale

B sus b9 arpeggio

C Lydian augmented scale

C maj #5 arpeggio

D Lydian dominant scale

D 7 #11 arpeggio

A Melodic minor/E scale

A minmaj7 /E arpeggio

F# Locrian #2 scale

F# min7 b5 arpeggio

G# Altered scale

G# Alt. arpeggio

4 Note Scale Groupings

The following exercise outlines the use of 4 note groupings moving stepwise diatonically through the scale of A melodic minor.

For example, the 4 note grouping starts on the root note or 1st degree of the scale and progresses stepwise . The exercise then descends from the 2nd octave A back to the root.

Ascending

Descending

Permutation 2 Up & Down

As in the previous exercise the following exercise outlines the use of 4 note groupings moving stepwise diatonically through the scale of A melodic minor.

Notice in exercise #2 the 4 note grouping starts on the root note or 1st degree of the scale and progresses stepwise. In this example we descend when we hit the 5th note in the sequence eg. descending from the 2nd 4 note grouping.

Ascending

Descending

Broken Thirds

Ascending

Descending

3 Note Groupings

A Melodic minor scale in triplet groupings
Ascending

Descending

Diatonic 7th Chords in Triplets

Starting on the Root
A min/maj7 arpeggio

Starting on the 2nd
B min7 arpeggio

Starting on the 3rd
C maj7/#5 arpeggio

Starting on the 4th
D 7#11 arpeggio

Starting on the 5th
E 7 arpeggio

Starting on the 6th
F# min7 b5 arpeggio

Starting on the 7th
G# min7 b5 arpeggio

Starting on the Root
A min/maj 7 arpeggio

4 Note Groupings Diatonic Triads

Ascending 1351

min min aug maj maj dim dim min

Descending 1351

min dim dim maj maj aug min min

Ascending 1531

min min aug maj maj dim dim min

Descending 1531

min dim dim maj maj aug min min

4 Note Groupings Diatonic 7th Chords

Ascending

Descending

Permutation 2
Ascending & descending

Permutation 3

Down the chord stepwise up the scale

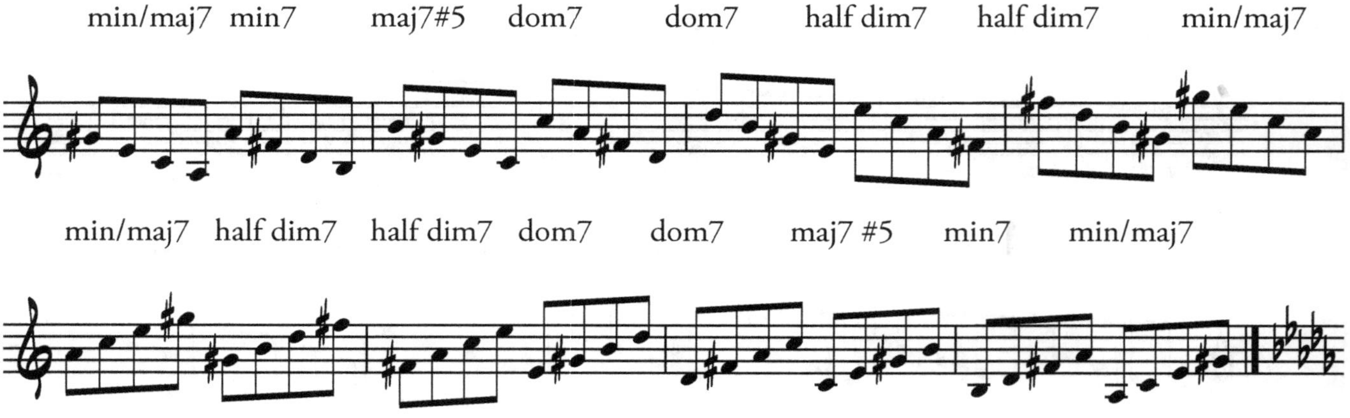

Scale studies in the key of Bb Melodic Minor

Scales, Modes and Arpeggios over 2 octaves

Bb Melodic minor scale

Bb min maj7 arpeggio

C sus b9 scale

C sus b9 arpeggio

Db Lydian augmented scale

Db maj #5 arpeggio

Eb Lydian dominant scale

Eb 7 #11 arpeggio

Bb Melodic minor/ F scale

Bb minmaj7 /F arpeggio

G Locrian #2 scale

G min7 b5 arpeggio

A Altered scale

A Alt. arpeggio

4 Note Scale Groupings

The following exercise outlines the use of 4 note groupings moving stepwise diatonically through the scale of Bb melodic minor.
For example, the 4 note grouping starts on the root note or 1st degree of the scale and progresses stepwise.
Theexercise then descends from the 2nd octave Bb back to the root.

Ascending

Descending

Permutation 2 Up & Down

As in the previous exercise the following exercise outlines the use of 4 note groupings moving stepwise diatonically through the scale of Bb melodic minor.

Notice in exercise #2 the 4 note grouping starts on the root note or 1st degree of the scale and progresses stepwise. In this example we descend when we hit the 5th note in the sequence eg. descending from the 2nd 4 note grouping.

Ascending

Descending

Broken Thirds

Ascending

Descending

3 Note Groupings

Bb Melodic minor scale in triplet groupings
Ascending

Descending

Diatonic 7th Chords in Triplets

Starting on the Root
Bb min/maj7 arpeggio

Starting on the 2nd
C min7 arpeggio

Starting on the 3rd
Db maj7/#5 arpeggio

Starting on the 4th
Eb 7#11 arpeggio

Starting on the 5th
F 7 arpeggio

Starting on the 6th
G min7 b5 arpeggio

Starting on the 7th
A min7 b5 arpeggio

Starting on the Root
Bb min/maj 7 arpeggio

4 Note Groupings Diatonic Triads

Ascending 1351

Descending 1351

Ascending 1531

Descending 1531

4 Note Groupings Diatonic 7th Chords

Ascending

min/maj7 min7 maj7#5 dom7 dom7 half dim7 half dim7 min/maj7

min7 maj7#5 dom7 dom7 half dim7 half dim7 min/maj7

Descending

min/maj7 half dim7 half dim7 dom7 dom7 maj7 #5 min7 min/maj7

half dim7 half dim7 dom7 dom7 maj7 #5 min7 min/maj7

Permutation 2
Ascending & descending

min/maj7 min7 maj7#5 dom7 dom7 half dim7 half dim7 min/maj7

half dim7 half dim7 dom7 dom7 maj7#5 min7 min/maj7

Permutation 3

Down the chord stepwise up the scale

Scale studies in the key of B Melodic Minor

Scales, Modes and Arpeggios over 2 octaves

B Melodic minor scale

B min maj7 arpeggio

C# sus b9 scale

C# sus b9 arpeggio

D Lydian augmented scale

D maj #5 arpeggio

E Lydian dominant scale

E 7 #11 arpeggio

C# Melodic minor/ F# scale

C# minmaj7 / F# arpeggio

G# Locrian #2 scale

G# min7 b5 arpeggio

A# Altered scale

A# Alt. arpeggio

4 Note Scale Groupings

The following exercise outlines the use of 4 note groupings moving stepwise diatonically through the scale of B melodic minor.
For example, the 4 note grouping starts on the root note or 1st degree of the scale and progresses stepwise . The exercise then descends from the 2nd octave B back to the root.

Ascending

Descending

Permutation 2 — Up & Down

As in the previous exercise the following exercise outlines the use of 4 note groupings moving stepwise diatonically through the scale of B melodic minor.
Notice in exercise #2 the 4 note grouping starts on the root note or 1st degree of the scale and progresses stepwise. In this example we descend when we hit the 5th note in the sequence eg. descending from the 2nd 4 note grouping.

Ascending

Descending

Broken Thirds

Ascending

Descending

3 Note Groupings

B Melodic minor scale in triplet groupings
Ascending

Descending

Diatonic 7th Chords in Triplets

Starting on the Root
B min/maj7 arpeggio

Starting on the 2nd
C# min7 arpeggio

Starting on the 3rd
D maj7/#5 arpeggio

Starting on the 4th
E 7#11 arpeggio

Starting on the 5th
F# 7 arpeggio

Starting on the 6th
G# min7 b5 arpeggio

Starting on the 7th
A# min7 b5 arpeggio

Starting on the Root
B min/maj 7 arpeggio

4 Note Groupings Diatonic Triads

Ascending 1351

min min aug maj maj dim dim min

Descending 1351

min dim dim maj maj aug min min

Ascending 1531

min min aug maj maj dim dim min

Descending 1531

min dim dim maj maj aug min min

4 Note Groupings Diatonic 7th Chords

Ascending

Descending

Permutation 2
Ascending & descending

Permutation 3
Down the chord stepwise up the scale

IN CONCLUSION ......

It has been a vast amount of work and dedicated practice that brings the guitarist to the last page of this book having covered all the examples within.
It has been the aim of the " Jazz Guitar Workshop " guitar book series to give the aspiring jazz guitarist a resource of scale related material in 12 keys which can be used to develop a dedicated daily practice routine.
Having covered the material in this book you are now well on your way to finding your own voice as a guitarist and as a musician.

Practice the exercises until they become familiar striving for good tone, time and articulation but most importantly - Listen to as much music as you can, Listen to the masters.

The objective has been to make the material for the student as easy to absorb as possible, as a confidance building mechanism.
Your thoughts and comments are important to us and assist us in providing future generations of musicians with quality educational material.

Please send youre thoughts or comments to info@jazzguitarworks.com

Other books in the series

Jazz Guitar Workshop

Daily Warm Up Exercises for Guitar - Guitar tab
by Robert Green
Jazz Guitar Workshop - 12 key Jazz Guitar Workout.
by Robert Green
Jazz Guitar Workshop - 12 key Jazz Guitar Workout
Harmonic Minor & Symmetric Scale Edition
by Robert Green

Coming Soon.
Jazz Guitar Workshop Book II

Jazz Guitar Workshop - Walking bass lines - The Blues in 12 keys Guitar tab
by Steven Mooney
Jazz Guitar Workshop - Walking bass lines - Rhythm changes in 12 keys Guitar tab
by Steven Mooney
Jazz Guitar Workshop - Walking bass lines - Standard Lines Guitar tab
by Steven Mooney

Follow us on the web at

Waterfallpublishinghouse.com

Jazzguitarworks.com

www.ingramcontent.com/pod-product-compliance
Lightning Source LLC
Chambersburg PA
CBHW081417090426
42738CB00017B/3399
* 9 7 8 1 9 3 7 1 8 7 0 7 1 *